FRACTIONS, GEOMETRY & COMPLEX MATH

D0506541

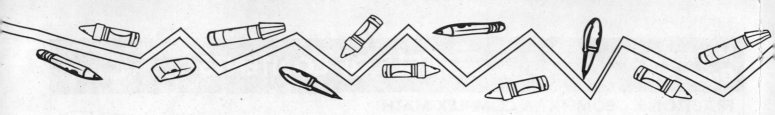

Mathematics Grade 5-6
Fractions, Geometry & Complex Math

Check your work with the Answer Key at the back of this book!

Materials You Will Need:

❏ A good pencil (or 2) with a working eraser

❏ Crayons

Benefits of Fractions, Geometry & Complex Math:

1. Practice multiplication & division!

2. Understand more about fractions & decimals

3. Use basic measurements & geometry strategies

4. Improve your understanding of probability and percents

Parent & Teacher Coaching Tips:

❏ *Prepare.* Provide your child with a quiet, well-lit place to study. Prepare a desk or table with an upright chair that is comfortable. Make sure that your child has plenty of room to work and spread out materials.

❏ *Schedule.* Set a study schedule. Choose a time that seems to work well for your child. Include your child in this study scheduling process and select a time when your child is well-rested and alert. Be sure to allow a break from working after a long school day.

❏ *Engage.* How does your child learn best? Use your child's learning strengths to reinforce information AND work on building new skills with your child. Encourage FUN through movement, play, acting, writing, drawing, singing, music, talking, thinking, and more while you work with your child.

❏ *Break.* Take frequent breaks from studying. Throughout the book, you will find review pages after each section of skills. When your child completes the section, use the Book Mark to mark your place in the book. Take a break and return to studying at your next scheduled time.

❏ *Relax!* Your role is critical in helping your child succeed with this workbook, at school, and with standardized tests. Be sure to help your child to: eat well, sleep well, practice deep-breathing techniques to relax, visualize success, and release energy in a physical way (running, walking, playing sports).

❏ *Talk.* Encourage your child to talk about feelings related to test-anxiety, help your child understand the need for tests AND stress the value of <u>real</u> learning that is not always obvious with test scores.

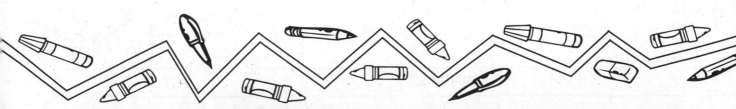

Name:_____   Date:_____

Write the correct answers.

1. Write the numerals in standard form.

   sixty-eight thousand, six _____

   eighteen thousand, four hundred ten _____

   one hundred eighty-nine thousand, three hundred fifty-two _____

   one million, seven thousand, nine hundred two _____

2. Write the numerals as decimals.

   four and two-tenths _____

   twelve and seven-tenths _____

   five and three-tenths _____

3. Write the numerals in word form.

   2,003 _____

   1,423,703 _____

   45,305 _____

   54.4 _____

   81.9 _____

4. Read the expanded form, then write the standard form of the numeral.

   $4,000 + 700 + 10 + 3$ _____ $10,000 + 6,000 + 900 + 20 + 3$ _____

   $5,000 + 200 + 40 + 9$ _____ $1,000,000 + 50,000 + 80 + 7$ _____

5. Mark an **X** on the hundreds place, circle the tens place, and draw a box around the tenths place in each numeral.

   1,286.7   85,203.1   544.91   3,988.5

6. Mark an **X** on the millions place, circle the thousands place, and draw a box around the hundreds place in each numeral.

   2,533,742.49   43,100,009.87   7,359,529.23   3,584,239.05

Name:_____ Date:_____

Write the value of the underlined digit.

68<u>1</u>

1,3<u>2</u>7

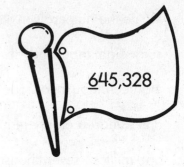

<u>6</u>45,328

1. ___8 tens___

2. _____

3. _____

<u>4</u>,897

46,231.7<u>8</u>

4. _____

5. _____

12.3<u>6</u>

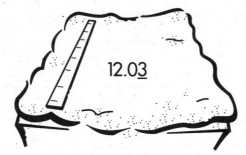

12.0<u>3</u>

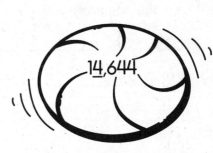

14,<u>6</u>44

6. _____

7. _____

8. _____

45,<u>1</u>02

<u>1</u>02,347

2,112.<u>6</u>8

<u>2</u>3,186

9. _____

10. _____

11. _____

12. _____

Name:_____   Date:_____

Write the correct answers.

1. Round the following numerals to the nearest ten.

527 _____   104 _____   955 _____   423 _____

2. Round the following numerals to the nearest hundred.

689 _____   527 _____   1,365 _____   421 _____

3. Round the following numerals to the nearest thousand.

1,365 _____   1,748 _____   5,231 _____   4,522 _____

4. Round the following numerals to the nearest tenth.

527.63 _____   289.34 _____   671.57 _____   15.85 _____

5. Estimate each sum or difference by rounding each numeral to the nearest hundred.

17,684 17,700	4,930	26,490	53,620
+ 35,419 +35,400	+ 9,407 + _____	+ 5,601 + _____	+ 14,760 + _____
53,100			

98,601	13,481	47,486	76,407
- 16,519 - _____	- 4,681 - _____	- 29,581 - _____	- 35,616 - _____

6. Estimate each sum or difference by rounding each numeral to the nearest thousand.

17,684 17,700	79,254	55,760	71,487
+ 35,419 +35,400	+ 43,601 + _____	+ 41,632 + _____	+26,418 + _____
53,100			

54,307	92,471	82,386	19,491
- 30,817 - _____	- 45,981 - _____	- 19,470 - _____	- 5,691 - _____

Finding an average is easy!

$$
\begin{array}{r}
86 \\
98 \\
+71 \\
\hline
255
\end{array}
\qquad
3\overline{)255} \quad \text{85 is the average!}
$$

Tip:
To find the average, add the numerals, then divide the sum by the number of addends.

The table shows the class averages of high school seniors.

Student	Average
Sue D.	94.6
Diane W.	94.7
Clay D.	98.5
Bill R.	95.1
Kelly F.	98.9
Ken M.	90.6

1. Put the averages in order from greatest to least.

   _____

2. If a seventh student were added to the list with an average of 90.9, where would his or her average be placed in the order?

   _____

3. Find the total average of the students.

   _____

---

4. Find the average of each girl's scores. _____

5. Who has the higher average? _____

6. How much of a difference is there between the averages?

   _____

Ruthie's math scores:
95, 83, 79, 97, 96, 91, 89, 90
Jean's math scores:
87, 78, 91, 99, 84, 91, 89, 100

---

7. Sarah works at a café in the village. Below are her tip totals for the past five days. Find the average.

   $10 $14 $13 $18 $20

   Average: _____

8. Look at the point amounts Chris scored during the past season's basketball games. Find the average of his points per game.

   24   32   27   40   18   33   Average: _____

   Compare it with his 34.7 average from the year before. What is the difference? Did Chris improve or not?

   _____

A **prime** number is only divisible by the number 1 and itself.
A **composite** number is divisible by more than 1 and itself.

The number 2 has only two factors, which are 1 and 2 (itself).
It is only divisible by these factors. Therefore, 2 is a **prime** number.

The number 4 has 1, 2, and 4 as factors, so it is divisible by
more than 1 and itself. Therefore, 4 is a **composite** number.

Look at each number. Write **P** if it is a **prime** number or **C** if it is a **composite** number. Circle the even numbers.

A. 9   22   5   17   51   42   73   13
   __C__   ___   ___   ___   ___   ___   ___   ___

B. 49   14   19   29   32   81   25   39
   ___   ___   ___   ___   ___   ___   ___   ___

C. 64   78   91   54   94   45   27   83
   ___   ___   ___   ___   ___   ___   ___   ___

D. 12   89   68   103   34   47   109   122
   ___   ___   ___   ___   ___   ___   ___   ___

E. 74   33   58   44   87   94   40   52
   ___   ___   ___   ___   ___   ___   ___   ___

F. 61   115   107   67   51   43   58   105
   ___   ___   ___   ___   ___   ___   ___   ___

G. 93   83   72   38   25   15   88   34
   ___   ___   ___   ___   ___   ___   ___   ___

Name:_____   Date:_____

Prime factorization is writing a composite number
as a product of prime factors.

To find the **prime factorization** of 24, only use prime numbers
as factors to equal 24.

Look! These numbers are prime!

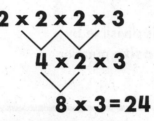

2 x 2 x 2 x 3

4 x 2 x 3

8 x 3 = 24

Draw a line to match the number to its **factorization**.
(Hint: The answers must be entirely in prime numbers.)

A. 72	• 2 x 5 x 5 • 2 x 36 • 2 x 2 x 2 x 3 x 3	D. 77	• 3 x 3 x 3 x 3 x 2 • 2 x 3 x 7 • 7 x 11
B. 81	• 3 x 3 x 3 x 3 • 3 x 3 x 3 x 7 • 3 x 3 x 5	E. 48	• 2 x 2 x 2 x 2 x 36 • 3 x 2 x 2 x 2 x 2 • 7 x 2 x 2
C. 36	• 3 x 3 x 3 x 9 • 2 x 2 x 5 • 2 x 2 x 3 x 3	F. 45	• 3 x 3 x 5 • 2 x 2 x 2 x 3 • 3 x 5

---

1. Write the **prime factorization** for the following numbers.

28_____   72_____

16_____   144_____

21_____   56_____

18_____   64_____

27_____   42_____

---

2. Find the product.

3 x 5 x 5 x 11 = _____   2 x 3 x 3 = _____   2 x 2 x 2 x 3 x 3 = _____

2 x 2 x 3 x 3 x 5 = _____   3 x 7 x 7 = _____   2 x 2 x 5 = _____

Name:_____   Date:_____

Review: Place Value & Number Form

1. Match the description to the correct number.

6 in the hundreds place	6,431.203
7 in the thousands place	45,662,871
3 in the thousandths place	104,623
6 in the ten thousands place	9,402,101.33
4 in the hundred thousands place	27,984.53
2 in the hundredths place	331,095
9 in the tens place	3,110.02

2. Write the following numbers in words.

6,294 _____

43,222 _____

561,364 _____

3. Write the following numbers in expanded form.

4,372 _____

94,355 _____

631,987 _____

4. Round the following numbers to the nearest hundred.

694 _____   435 _____   2,398 _____   5,553 _____

5. Round the following numbers to the nearest thousand.

2,436 _____   2,987 _____   4,561 _____   9,911 _____

Name:_____   Date:_____

Review: Prime & Composite Numbers & Averages

1. Circle the letter **P** if the number is **prime** and **C** if it is **composite**.

17	27	49	83	64	67
P C	P C	P C	P C	P C	P C

25	89	44	109	99	107
P C	P C	P C	P C	P C	P C

2. Write the **prime factorization** for the following numbers.

18 _____   64 _____

42 _____   27 _____

3. Find the **average** for each group of numbers.

12, 13, 14, 15, 16, 17, 18 _____   85, 92, 93, 87, 90, 81 _____

27, 12, 59, 23, 47, 66, 18 _____   102, 113, 125, 176, 144 _____

TAKE A BREAK! You did a great job! Place your Book Mark here & RELAX!

Name:_____   Date:_____

Multiply. Then, write the letter next to each product on the correct lines below to reveal the secret message. Not all letters will be used.

63 x 4 **D**	22 x 3 **S**	50 x 6 **O**	78 x 7 **!**
50 x 2 **K**	36 x 9 **I**	92 x 3 **U**	24 x 5 **D**
85 x 5 **I**	97 x 8 **Y**	47 x 6 **T**	38 x 6 **M**
94 x 8 **N**	53 x 9 **E**	37 x 5 **B**	64 x 4 **C**

776   300   276   120   324   252   425   282   546

Name:_____   Date:_____

Multiply. Then, use the code to color the picture.

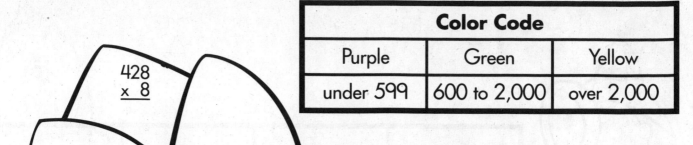

Color Code		
Purple	Green	Yellow
under 599	600 to 2,000	over 2,000

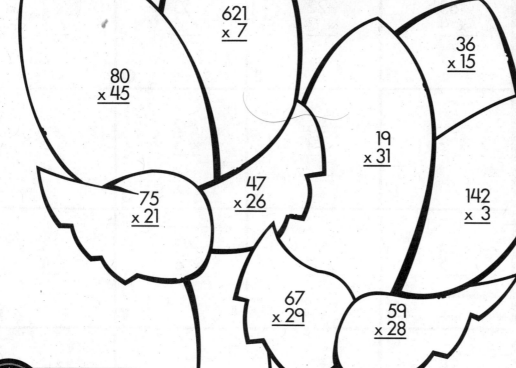

428
x 8

621
x 7

36
x 15

80
x 45

19
x 31

75
x 21

47
x 26

142
x 3

67
x 29

59
x 28

221
x 6

44
x 34

 Challenge: On another sheet of paper, write the prime factorization for each of your answers on this page.

Tip: Use the area around the picture to solve equations, or use a piece of scratch paper!

Multiplying by 1- and 2-digit numbers

Name:_____   Date:_____

Multiply.

A. 335   468   608   843
   x 34   x 23   x 19   x 10

B. 879   419   224   310
   x 92   x 41   x 16   x 99

C. 479   718   617   518
   x 18   x 39   x 25   x 29

D. 244   197   167   718   517
   x 16   x 31   x 76   x 13   x 49

E. 732   577   833   619   729
   x 50   x 65   x 16   x 51   x 23

F. 918   419   245   413   189
   x 43   x 23   x 91   x 43   x 17

```
  2 1 1
2,432
x   16
14592
+ 24320  ← Add a zero because you're
          multiplying in the tens place.
38,912
```

Multiply.

A. 4,617   6,704   2,280   8,689   6,351
    x   19   x   25   x   12   x   56   x   41

B. 6,281   1,579   5,724   1,926   7,813
    x   29   x   27   x   34   x   37   x   83

C. 5,117   3,410   1,039   4,759   8,348
    x   46   x   57   x   76   x   75   x   44

D. 6,912   5,458   3,332   5,685   7,315
    x   18   x   47   x   24   x   93   x   64

E. 8,005   4,798   6,201   3,029   5,652
    x   34   x   72   x   49   x   99   x   26

263
x 146
1578
10520 ←— Add a zero because you're multiplying in the tens place.
+ 26300 ←— Add two zeroes because you're multiplying in the hundreds place.
38,398

Three times the fun!

Multiply.

A. 126   325   401   836   406
   x 158   x 122   x 241   x 425   x 134

B. 227   531   200   637   342
   x 114   x 289   x 146   x 741   x 300

C. 476   512   339   741   874
   x 220   x 478   x 157   x 335   x 209

D. 986   678   425   507   805
   x 608   x 385   x 227   x 524   x 775

Name:_____   Date:_____

Divide. Then, draw a line to the matching quotients.

A. 4⟌4,123   67 r3

B. 3⟌914   58 r6

C. 7⟌7,656   304 r2

D. 9⟌606   1,030 r3

E. 8⟌470   1,093 r5

F. 6⟌321   128 r2

G. 5⟌642   748 r1

H. 7⟌426   53 r3

I. 7⟌3,478   60 r6

J. 2⟌1,497   496 r6

Help! I can't find the match.

Challenge: Have a friend or family member make up more division equations for you to practice. See how quickly you can find the correct answers!

Name:_____ Date:_____

Divide.

A.
$$\begin{array}{r} 52r8 \\ 16\overline{)840} \\ -80\downarrow \\ \hline 40 \\ -32 \\ \hline 8 \end{array}$$
  $12\overline{)670}$ $12\overline{)905}$

Now you are dividing with remainders.

B. $15\overline{)984}$ $36\overline{)795}$

C. $36\overline{)592}$ $45\overline{)976}$ $40\overline{)862}$ $23\overline{)860}$ $21\overline{)780}$

D. $14\overline{)294}$ $37\overline{)783}$ $43\overline{)917}$ $19\overline{)276}$ $16\overline{)984}$

E. $26\overline{)848}$ $14\overline{)881}$ $18\overline{)454}$ $21\overline{)883}$ $20\overline{)495}$

F. $22\overline{)871}$ $13\overline{)633}$ $20\overline{)877}$ $38\overline{)982}$ $18\overline{)537}$

Name:_____   Date:_____

Divide. Then, use the code to solve the riddle.

Letter Code		
2 r38 = –	12 = o	21 = k
3 r30 = q	15 = t	23 = e
5 r4 = s	16 = h	27 = p
6 = !	19 = r	28 r6 = m
7 = a	20 r7 = l	29 r7 = i

At which store did the dog lose its tail?

At the

19 44⟌4,123	36⟌828	54⟌146	29⟌435	21⟌147	18⟌529	15⟌307
r						

42⟌214	16⟌256	53⟌636	34⟌918	40⟌240

Name:_____ Date:_____

Divide.

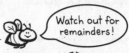

Watch out for remainders!

A.
$$
\begin{array}{r}
22 \\
51\overline{)1{,}122} \\
-102 \\
\hline
102 \\
-102 \\
\hline
0
\end{array}
$$
     $45\overline{)1{,}578}$ $24\overline{)1{,}261}$ $82\overline{)6{,}198}$ $40\overline{)1{,}080}$

B. $37\overline{)1{,}068}$ $84\overline{)1{,}398}$ $86\overline{)1{,}290}$ $66\overline{)5{,}637}$ $27\overline{)1{,}641}$

C. $26\overline{)1{,}170}$ $73\overline{)1{,}846}$ $31\overline{)1{,}736}$ $82\overline{)6{,}729}$ $93\overline{)1{,}368}$

D. $9{,}659 \div 34 =$ _____ $7{,}506 \div 51 =$ _____

E. $8{,}608 \div 30 =$ _____ $7{,}501 \div 14 =$ _____

Name:_____   Date:_____

Read each problem. Then, divide or multiply to solve it.

Tip:
If you are having difficulty with any of these problems, draw pictures to help you do the math.

1. Johnny needs to buy chicken for a Mexican fiesta. He can buy seven packages of chicken for $26.25. How much does each package of chicken cost?

2. Katie needs cucumbers for a salad. She bought five cucumbers for $2.55. What is the cost per cucumber?

3. A grocery store clerk stacked cereal boxes in rows of 40 across on a shelf. He made six rows of boxes. How many boxes of cereal were stacked in all?

4. Mrs. Smith buys three cases of juice boxes for her fifth grade class. Each case costs $2.50 and contains 12 juice boxes. How much does Mrs. Smith pay for all the juice?

5. Julie and her friends go to the store. Julie has $40.00 that she wants to share equally with her seven friends. How much money does each girl get?

6. Abbey and her friends decide to buy five bags of candy. There were 45 pieces of candy in each bag. What is the total number of pieces that Abbey and her friends shared?

Name:_____   Date:_____

Review: Multiplication

Multiply.

A.
$$198 \times 73$$
$$1{,}462 \times 30$$
$$2{,}432 \times 23$$
$$1{,}665 \times 79$$
$$3{,}913 \times 77$$
$$174 \times 36$$

B.
$$173 \times 72$$
$$1{,}643 \times 65$$
$$345 \times 544$$
$$415 \times 46$$
$$654 \times 173$$
$$3{,}346 \times 94$$

C.
$$354 \times 13$$
$$982 \times 70$$
$$491 \times 243$$
$$2{,}651 \times 63$$
$$1{,}531 \times 61$$
$$9{,}879 \times 75$$

D.
$$6{,}462 \times 36$$
$$5{,}413 \times 73$$
$$5{,}459 \times 94$$
$$879 \times 83$$
$$563 \times 61$$
$$163 \times 39$$

E.
$$9{,}963 \times 143$$
$$4{,}563 \times 261$$
$$428 \times 363$$
$$539 \times 443$$
$$1{,}569 \times 296$$
$$255 \times 50$$

Name:_____   Date:_____

Review: Division

Multiply.

A. 6)240   2)5,436   35)5,257   6)1,224   4)573   6)513

B. 3)7,564   9)1,278   12)2,436   8)2,768   16)347   3)173

C. 16)1,664   18)2,250   4)3,412   19)361   38)344   9)512

D. 13)3,302   3)6,150   19)8,550   12)420   45)287   21)7,413

E. 8)439   13)3,413   9)373   15)870   2)6,910   14)2,439

STOP! TAKE A BREAK! **You did a great job!** Place your Book Mark here & RELAX!

Write the answers.

1. How many pieces of fruit are in the whole set? _____

2. What fraction of the set do the bananas represent? _____

3. What fraction of the set do the apples represent? _____

4. What fraction of the set do the pineapples represent? _____

5. What fraction of the set do the pears represent? _____

6. What fraction of the set do the oranges represent? _____

7. Which fruit makes up $\frac{1}{3}$ of the set? _____

8. Which fruit makes up $\frac{1}{6}$ of the set? _____

9. Which two combinations of fruit make up one half of the set?

_____ and _____

Name:_____   Date:_____

Find the sum or difference in its simplest form.

A. $\dfrac{8}{18} - \dfrac{2}{18} = \dfrac{6}{18} = \dfrac{1}{3}$ $\dfrac{9}{24} - \dfrac{5}{24} =$

B. $\dfrac{7}{13} - \dfrac{5}{13} =$ $\dfrac{7}{18} - \dfrac{2}{18} =$

C. $\dfrac{1}{8} + \dfrac{7}{8} =$ $\dfrac{20}{32} + \dfrac{12}{32} =$

D. $\dfrac{10}{20} - \dfrac{5}{20} =$ $\dfrac{22}{30} + \dfrac{3}{30} =$

E. $\dfrac{8}{32} + \dfrac{14}{32} =$ $\dfrac{9}{18} + \dfrac{9}{18} =$

F. $\dfrac{14}{26} + \dfrac{12}{26} =$ $\dfrac{13}{22} + \dfrac{9}{22} =$

G. $\dfrac{24}{40} - \dfrac{8}{40} =$ $\dfrac{9}{30} - \dfrac{3}{30} =$

H. $\dfrac{14}{28} - \dfrac{7}{28} =$ $\dfrac{24}{42} - \dfrac{10}{42} =$

Action!

Adding Fractions with Common Denominators

Fractions that have a common denominator are called **like fractions**.

Solve the problems.

1. Carla walked $\dfrac{7}{8}$ of a mile on Monday, $\dfrac{6}{8}$ mile on Tuesday, and $\dfrac{4}{8}$ of a mile on Wednesday. How far did Carla walk in all?

2. Joey swam the butterfly stroke for $\dfrac{7}{10}$ of a mile and freestyle for $\dfrac{8}{10}$ of a mile. How far did Joey swim in all?

3. On Tuesday, Olivia and her friend pedaled $2\dfrac{3}{4}$ of a mile. Wednesday, they increased their mileage by $1\dfrac{2}{4}$ of a mile. How far did they pedal over both days?

4. This week Jenny bought fabric for two dresses. One dress required $3\dfrac{5}{8}$ yards of fabric and the other called for $4\dfrac{5}{8}$ yards. How much fabric did Jenny buy in all?

Challenge: When you have found your answer in yards, convert the yards into feet. Then, convert the feet into inches.

Adding and subtracting fractions with common denominators

To add or subtract fractions with different denominators, find the **least common multiple (LCM)** of each denominator, which then becomes the **lowest common denominator (LCD)**. To add $\frac{2}{3} + \frac{1}{4}$, find the **LCM** of both denominators.

Multiples of 3: 3, 6, 9, **12**, 15
Multiples of 4: 4, 8, **12**, 16

12 is the **LCM**, so it becomes the **LCD** in the equation.

$$\frac{2}{3} \frac{(\times 4)}{(\times 4)} = \frac{8}{\mathbf{12}}$$

$$\frac{1}{4} \frac{(\times 3)}{(\times 3)} = \frac{3}{\mathbf{12}}$$

$$\frac{8}{12} + \frac{3}{12} = \frac{11}{\mathbf{12}}$$

Find the **LCM/LCD** for each pair of fractions and convert to like fractions. Add.

A. $\frac{2}{4} + \frac{6}{6}$	$\frac{2}{5} + \frac{4}{10}$
B. $\frac{7}{8} + \frac{3}{4}$	$\frac{2}{3} + \frac{3}{4}$
C. $\frac{4}{7} + \frac{2}{3}$	$\frac{5}{6} + \frac{7}{8}$
D. $\frac{7}{9} + \frac{1}{6}$	$\frac{3}{7} + \frac{1}{2}$
E. $\frac{3}{6} + \frac{1}{4}$	$\frac{5}{6} + \frac{4}{8}$
F. $\frac{2}{8} + \frac{2}{6}$	$\frac{1}{3} + \frac{3}{6}$
G. $\frac{1}{2} + \frac{3}{5}$	$\frac{3}{5} + \frac{1}{3}$
H. $\frac{3}{4} + \frac{1}{2}$	$\frac{1}{9} + \frac{1}{5}$

Name:_____   Date:_____

Add the fractions. Then, simplify the sum if you can.

Tip:
Find the lowest common denominator first. Convert to like fractions and solve.

A. $\dfrac{2}{5} + \dfrac{1}{3} =$ $\dfrac{6}{15} + \dfrac{5}{15} = \dfrac{11}{15}$	$\dfrac{4}{7} + \dfrac{2}{4} =$	$\dfrac{7}{9} + \dfrac{1}{2} =$
B. $\dfrac{5}{6} + \dfrac{2}{5} =$	$\dfrac{2}{3} + \dfrac{1}{4} =$	$\dfrac{4}{6} + \dfrac{5}{8} =$
C. $\dfrac{8}{10} + \dfrac{4}{5} =$	$\dfrac{2}{3} + \dfrac{5}{6} =$	$\dfrac{7}{9} + \dfrac{1}{3} =$
D. $\dfrac{4}{12} + \dfrac{3}{8} =$	$\dfrac{4}{5} + \dfrac{1}{3} =$	$\dfrac{8}{15} + \dfrac{5}{6} =$
E. $\dfrac{9}{11} + \dfrac{1}{2} =$	$\dfrac{7}{15} + \dfrac{4}{6} =$	$\dfrac{1}{5} + \dfrac{5}{6} =$
F. $\dfrac{4}{5} + \dfrac{7}{8} =$	$\dfrac{9}{15} + \dfrac{4}{9} =$	$\dfrac{7}{18} + \dfrac{3}{4} =$

Adding fractions with unlike denominators; simplifying fractions

Challenge: Use a pair of dice to make up your own equations to practice. Roll the dice and write the smaller number on top and the larger number on the bottom of a fraction. Roll again, write the next fraction, then add or subtract your fractions.

Add and subtract the fractions.
Then, simplify the answer if you can.

A.	$\frac{7}{8} - \frac{1}{2} =$ $\frac{7}{8} - \frac{4}{8} = \frac{3}{8}$	$\frac{6}{7} - \frac{2}{3} =$	$\frac{7}{9} - \frac{1}{4} =$	$\frac{6}{8} - \frac{2}{4} =$
B.	$\frac{11}{15} - \frac{3}{5} =$	$\frac{5}{6} - \frac{2}{8} =$	$\frac{5}{7} - \frac{2}{4} =$	$\frac{11}{15} - \frac{2}{5} =$
C.	$\frac{13}{15} - \frac{4}{6} =$	$\frac{7}{12} - \frac{4}{9} =$	$\frac{9}{10} - \frac{7}{15} =$	$\frac{10}{25} - \frac{5}{20} =$
D.	$\frac{5}{6} - \frac{1}{3} =$	$\frac{4}{5} - \frac{1}{3} =$	$\frac{8}{11} - \frac{1}{4} =$	$\frac{4}{8} - \frac{2}{16} =$
E.	$\frac{3}{9} - \frac{2}{6} =$	$\frac{2}{3} - \frac{2}{7} =$	$\frac{8}{15} - \frac{2}{5} =$	$\frac{3}{9} - \frac{1}{3} =$
F.	$\frac{6}{8} - \frac{2}{3} =$	$\frac{9}{18} - \frac{2}{3} =$	$\frac{13}{14} - \frac{3}{7} =$	$\frac{7}{9} - \frac{5}{36} =$

Convert to **like fractions**, then compare using the symbols <, =, or >. Circle each fraction whose value is greater than $\frac{1}{2}$.

Comparing fractions is easier when they are like.

A. $\frac{5}{8} \square \frac{4}{12}$ $\boxed{\frac{15}{24}} > \frac{8}{24}$ $\frac{5}{6} \square \frac{3}{9}$

B. $\frac{4}{12} \square \frac{3}{6}$ $\frac{3}{7} \square \frac{2}{3}$

C. $\frac{7}{10} \square \frac{3}{4}$ $\frac{9}{12} \square \frac{3}{8}$

D. $\frac{3}{5} \square \frac{2}{4}$ $\frac{3}{4} \square \frac{2}{3}$ $\frac{1}{3} \square \frac{5}{6}$

E. $\frac{10}{12} \square \frac{2}{3}$ $\frac{1}{4} \square \frac{3}{7}$ $\frac{2}{6} \square \frac{2}{3}$

F. $\frac{4}{9} \square \frac{1}{2}$ $\frac{8}{15} \square \frac{5}{6}$ $\frac{7}{9} \square \frac{2}{3}$

G. $\frac{7}{8} \square \frac{2}{3}$ $\frac{7}{8} \square \frac{1}{2}$ $\frac{5}{8} \square \frac{2}{4}$

H. $\frac{3}{5} \square \frac{1}{2}$ $\frac{4}{9} \square \frac{1}{3}$ $\frac{4}{8} \square \frac{3}{6}$

Convert to **like fractions**, then put them in order from least to greatest.

I. $\frac{1}{9}, \frac{1}{12}, \frac{1}{6}$ _____ $\frac{3}{16}, \frac{1}{8}, \frac{3}{4}$ _____

J. $\frac{6}{12}, \frac{5}{6}, \frac{2}{9}$ _____ $\frac{4}{5}, \frac{2}{10}, \frac{9}{15}$ _____

K. $\frac{7}{12}, \frac{5}{6}, \frac{2}{4}$ _____ $\frac{2}{3}, \frac{1}{5}, \frac{8}{10}$ _____

Converting and comparing like fractions; ordering fractions

To add mixed numerals, find the lowest common denominator. Then, add the whole number and the numerators.

$$5\frac{4}{7} + 3\frac{1}{3} = 5\frac{12}{21} + 3\frac{7}{21} = 8\frac{19}{21}$$

To subtract mixed numerals, find the lowest common denominator, too. Sometimes, you will need to regroup.

$$5\frac{3}{4} - 2\frac{5}{6} = 5\frac{9}{12} - 2\frac{10}{12}$$

Regroup 1 whole, or 12 parts, from the whole number 5.
Add the 12 parts to your numerator, 9.

$$5\frac{9}{12} = 4\frac{21}{12}$$

$$4\frac{21}{12} - 2\frac{10}{12} = 2\frac{11}{12}$$

Solve the problems.

A. $4\frac{2}{3} + 3\frac{1}{4} =$ $6\frac{4}{7} + 8\frac{1}{3} =$ $7\frac{3}{8} + 2\frac{8}{12} =$

B. $6\frac{2}{3} + 3\frac{3}{4} =$ $9\frac{4}{5} - 7\frac{2}{3} =$ $12\frac{4}{9} - 4\frac{5}{6} =$

C. $14\frac{4}{6} + 3\frac{5}{8} =$ $7\frac{4}{12} + 4\frac{3}{6} =$ $5\frac{4}{5} + 2\frac{1}{3} =$

D. $7\frac{4}{5} - 4\frac{1}{4} =$ $10\frac{4}{8} - 4\frac{5}{6} =$ $12\frac{4}{8} - 3\frac{4}{5} =$

E. $10\frac{1}{2} + 5\frac{2}{8} =$ $9\frac{4}{16} + 3\frac{5}{8} =$ $2\frac{7}{9} + 4\frac{1}{2} =$

$\frac{3}{8} \times \frac{4}{5} = \frac{\mathbf{12}}{\mathbf{40}}$ ← —— Multiply the numerators.
⟵ —— Multiply the denominator.

Then, simplify the answer if you can.

$$\frac{\mathbf{12}}{\mathbf{40}} = \frac{\mathbf{3}}{\mathbf{10}}$$

It's multiplying!

Multiply the fractions. Then, simplify the product if you can.

A. $\frac{5}{6} \times \frac{7}{8} =$	$\frac{4}{5} \times \frac{6}{7} =$	$\frac{7}{9} \times \frac{4}{5} =$	$\frac{8}{9} \times \frac{2}{3} =$
B. $\frac{4}{8} \times \frac{3}{5} =$	$\frac{9}{10} \times \frac{2}{7} =$	$\frac{5}{7} \times \frac{9}{11} =$	$\frac{6}{9} \times \frac{2}{6} =$
C. $\frac{4}{6} \times \frac{7}{9} =$	$\frac{3}{6} \times \frac{7}{10}$	$\frac{4}{7} \times \frac{2}{3} =$	$\frac{5}{8} \times \frac{7}{9} =$
D. $\frac{6}{12} \times \frac{1}{2} =$	$\frac{3}{4} \times \frac{7}{8} =$	$\frac{3}{4} \times \frac{6}{7} =$	$\frac{5}{9} \times \frac{4}{10} =$
E. $\frac{1}{11} \times \frac{4}{5} =$	$\frac{8}{10} \times \frac{4}{6} =$	$\frac{3}{9} \times \frac{2}{3} =$	$\frac{4}{6} \times \frac{5}{4} =$
F. $\frac{4}{6} \times \frac{3}{12} =$	$\frac{3}{9} \times \frac{7}{8} =$	$\frac{1}{4} \times \frac{3}{6} =$	$\frac{8}{9} \times \frac{1}{3} =$

An easy recipe for multiplying whole numbers by fractions.

$$6 \times \frac{3}{4} = 6 \times \frac{3}{3} = \frac{6}{1} \times \frac{3}{4} = \frac{18}{4} = 4\frac{2}{4} = 4\frac{1}{2}$$

Take the whole number 6.
Place a 1 under it to make it a fraction.
Then, multiply the fractions.
For a well-done product, remember to make the fraction proper and simplify!

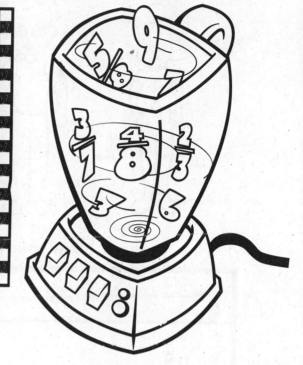

Multiply.

A. $5 \times \frac{3}{4} = $ _____ $8 \times \frac{1}{3} = $ _____ $7 \times \frac{4}{9} = $ _____

B. $9 \times \frac{3}{5} = $ _____ $4 \times \frac{1}{2} = $ _____ $6 \times \frac{2}{5} = $ _____

C. $4 \times \frac{2}{9} = $ _____ $2 \times \frac{4}{12} = $ _____ $5 \times \frac{4}{16} = $ _____

D. $3 \times \frac{5}{7} = $ _____ $7 \times \frac{4}{15} = $ _____ $8 \times \frac{4}{5} = $ _____

E. $10 \times \frac{3}{15} = $ _____ $12 \times \frac{3}{6} = $ _____ $7 \times \frac{4}{7} = $ _____

F. What is $\frac{1}{9}$ of 45? _____   What is $\frac{1}{4}$ of 16? _____

G. What is $\frac{1}{4}$ of 20? _____   What is $\frac{3}{8}$ of 4? _____

H. What is $\frac{2}{3}$ of 8? _____   What is $\frac{1}{8}$ of 26? _____

 ÷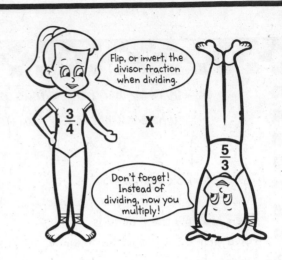

Flip, or invert, the divisor fraction when dividing.

Don't forget! Instead of dividing, now you multiply!

Divide the fractions. Show your work.

A. $\dfrac{4}{6} \div \dfrac{1}{3} = \dfrac{4}{6} \times \dfrac{3}{1} = \dfrac{12}{1} = 2$	$\dfrac{5}{7} \div \dfrac{2}{3} =$
B. $\dfrac{6}{8} \div \dfrac{4}{5} =$	$\dfrac{5}{9} \div \dfrac{2}{7} =$
C. $\dfrac{5}{8} \div \dfrac{2}{6} =$	$\dfrac{3}{6} \div \dfrac{2}{7} =$
D. $\dfrac{8}{10} \div \dfrac{3}{6} =$	$\dfrac{3}{5} \div \dfrac{1}{2} =$
E. $\dfrac{3}{4} \div \dfrac{1}{5} =$	$\dfrac{4}{8} \div \dfrac{1}{3} =$
F. $\dfrac{1}{3} \div \dfrac{1}{4} =$	$\dfrac{1}{4} \div \dfrac{4}{5} =$
G. $\dfrac{4}{9} \div \dfrac{2}{6} =$	$\dfrac{7}{9} \div \dfrac{3}{6} =$
H. $\dfrac{3}{5} \div \dfrac{4}{7} =$	$\dfrac{2}{4} \div \dfrac{1}{3} =$
I. $\dfrac{9}{10} \div \dfrac{3}{4} =$	
J. $\dfrac{6}{8} \div \dfrac{7}{9} =$	
K. $\dfrac{3}{5} \div \dfrac{4}{8} =$	
L. $\dfrac{6}{9} \div \dfrac{1}{4} =$	

This is a reciprocal.

Name:_____   Date:_____

Review: Fractions

Add or subtract.

A. $\dfrac{5}{6} + \dfrac{5}{8} =$ ____ $\dfrac{13}{21} + \dfrac{5}{7} =$ ____ $\dfrac{5}{6} + \dfrac{10}{18} =$ ____ $\dfrac{6}{7} + \dfrac{8}{9} =$ ____

B. $\dfrac{4}{5} + \dfrac{9}{15} =$ ____ $\dfrac{5}{16} + \dfrac{17}{8} =$ ____ $\dfrac{13}{12} + \dfrac{7}{8} =$ ____ $\dfrac{14}{24} + \dfrac{7}{12} =$ ____

C. $\dfrac{27}{30} - \dfrac{5}{6} =$ ____ $\dfrac{5}{6} - \dfrac{1}{5} =$ ____ $\dfrac{7}{8} - \dfrac{1}{2} =$ ____ $\dfrac{5}{6} - \dfrac{2}{9} =$ ____

D. $\dfrac{9}{16} - \dfrac{3}{8} =$ ____ $\dfrac{4}{5} - \dfrac{2}{8} =$ ____ $\dfrac{4}{7} - \dfrac{3}{14} =$ ____ $\dfrac{3}{4} - \dfrac{1}{5} =$ ____

E. $\dfrac{3}{6} - \dfrac{2}{15} =$ ____ $\dfrac{5}{8} - \dfrac{1}{6} =$ ____ $\dfrac{7}{9} - \dfrac{2}{6} =$ ____ $\dfrac{7}{24} - \dfrac{3}{12} =$ ____

F. $2\dfrac{1}{8} + 4\dfrac{1}{2} =$ ____ $3\dfrac{1}{2} + 5\dfrac{3}{6} =$ ____ $3\dfrac{9}{10} + 2\dfrac{4}{15} =$ ____ $2\dfrac{2}{3} + 3\dfrac{1}{6} =$ ____

G. $3\dfrac{7}{9} + 2\dfrac{3}{27} =$ ____ $4\dfrac{2}{8} + 3\dfrac{4}{16} =$ ____ $3\dfrac{2}{12} + 3\dfrac{1}{3} =$ ____ $6\dfrac{4}{9} + 2\dfrac{2}{3} =$ ____

H. $6\dfrac{7}{8} + \dfrac{2}{6} =$ ____ $6 + 3\dfrac{5}{9} =$ ____ $\dfrac{3}{12} + 5\dfrac{9}{12} =$ ____ $12\dfrac{4}{8} + \dfrac{2}{4} =$ ____

Compare. Use >, <, of =.

I. $5\dfrac{1}{4} - 1\dfrac{1}{8}$ ☐ $5\dfrac{4}{6} - 1\dfrac{1}{3}$ $6\dfrac{5}{18} + 1\dfrac{3}{9}$ ☐ $3\dfrac{1}{4} + 3\dfrac{4}{6}$ $\dfrac{6}{12}$ ☐ $\dfrac{9}{24}$

J. $7\dfrac{1}{2} - 4$ ☐ $9 - 7\dfrac{4}{10}$ $8\dfrac{7}{9} - 4\dfrac{1}{3}$ ☐ $9\dfrac{5}{6} + 5\dfrac{2}{3}$ $\dfrac{10}{21}$ ☐ $\dfrac{5}{7}$

K. $9 + 3\dfrac{4}{5}$ ☐ $15 - 4\dfrac{2}{3}$ $9\dfrac{4}{10} + 2\dfrac{3}{5}$ ☐ $10 + 3\dfrac{4}{9}$ $\dfrac{5}{15}$ ☐ $\dfrac{2}{3}$

L. $7\dfrac{1}{4} - 2\dfrac{2}{8}$ ☐ $3\dfrac{5}{8} - 1\dfrac{1}{3}$ $4\dfrac{7}{18} + 1\dfrac{3}{9}$ ☐ $2\dfrac{1}{2} + 3\dfrac{1}{2}$ $\dfrac{3}{12}$ ☐ $\dfrac{4}{8}$

Write the missing number.

M. $5\dfrac{2}{9} +$ _____ $= 11$ _____ $- 3\dfrac{2}{7} = 7\dfrac{5}{21}$ _____ $+ 2\dfrac{2}{3} = 5\dfrac{5}{6}$

N. _____ $- 6\dfrac{3}{5} = 3\dfrac{1}{3}$ _____ $- 7\dfrac{1}{6} = 4\dfrac{2}{3}$ _____ $- 5\dfrac{3}{4} = 9\dfrac{5}{8}$

Name:_____ Date:_____

Review: Fractions

Multiply. Then, simplify if you can.

A. $\frac{1}{3} \times \frac{5}{7} =$ _____ $\frac{2}{5} \times \frac{2}{6} =$ _____ $\frac{4}{8} \times \frac{5}{9} =$ _____ $\frac{5}{6} \times \frac{3}{4} =$ _____

B. $\frac{3}{5} \times \frac{4}{9} =$ _____ $\frac{5}{4} \times \frac{1}{2} =$ _____ $\frac{7}{8} \times \frac{8}{9} =$ _____ $\frac{3}{9} \times \frac{7}{10} =$ _____

C. $\frac{4}{9} \times 14 =$ _____ $\frac{7}{11} \times 9 =$ _____ $\frac{6}{9} \times 13 =$ _____ $22 \times \frac{1}{9} =$ _____

D. $\frac{3}{12} \times \frac{1}{2} =$ _____ $\frac{2}{15} \times \frac{1}{2} =$ _____ $\frac{4}{9} \times \frac{5}{6} =$ _____ $\frac{4}{8} \times \frac{1}{2} =$ _____

Divide. Then, simplify if you can.

F. $\frac{5}{9} \div \frac{1}{2} =$ _____ $\frac{4}{7} \div \frac{3}{4} =$ _____ $\frac{3}{7} \div \frac{5}{6} =$ _____ $\frac{8}{10} \div \frac{2}{9} =$ _____

G. $\frac{3}{4} \div \frac{4}{6} =$ _____ $\frac{2}{9} \div \frac{5}{6} =$ _____ $\frac{3}{6} \div \frac{2}{9} =$ _____ $\frac{5}{14} \div \frac{1}{18} =$ _____

H. $\frac{8}{9} \div \frac{5}{7} =$ _____ $\frac{3}{12} \div \frac{7}{10} =$ _____ $\frac{4}{16} \div \frac{2}{3} =$ _____ $14 \div \frac{4}{5} =$ _____

I. $\frac{5}{13} \div \frac{3}{5} =$ _____ $\frac{7}{12} \div \frac{6}{10} =$ _____ $\frac{3}{5} \div \frac{3}{8} =$ _____ $\frac{12}{16} \div \frac{1}{2} =$ _____

Solve.

1. Allen wants to cut a board that is $6\frac{3}{4}$ feet long into $\frac{1}{2}$ foot sections. How many sections can he cut?

2. If Jackie runs $\frac{9}{10}$ of a mile every day, how many miles will she run in two weeks?

   How many miles will she run if she doubles the length of her daily run?

STOP! TAKE A BREAK! You did a great job! Place your Book Mark here & RELAX!

Name:_____   Date:_____

Use the place value chart at the right to help you name **decimal** values.

←— **decimal** places —→

hundreds	tens	ones	decimal point	tenths	hundredths	thousandths	ten-thousandths	hundred-thousandths	millionths
2	1	7	.	5	3	9	4		

Let's get this straight.

The number **217.5394** is read as "two hundred seventeen and five thousand, three hundred ninety-four ten-thousandths."

Tip:
Do not write a comma between place values for the numerals after the **decimal** point.

1. Write the place value of the last digit in each number.

6.7328 _____   4.395 _____

43.39 _____   2.43893 _____

0.514 _____   13.81573 _____

2. Write each numeral in written form. Don't forget to use "and."

23.7 _____

2.49 _____

1.297 _____

1.0005 _____

21.006 _____

3.00009 _____

0.984 _____

3. Write each number in standard form.

fourteen and nine-tenths _____   nine and ten-thousandths _____

six hundred fifty and seven-thousandths _____   ninety-one and four-thousandths _____

eighty-four and seven-hundredths _____   one and nine-millionths _____

Understanding decimals; identifying decimal place values

Name:_____ Date:_____

The same amount can be written as a fraction or a **decimal**.

$$0.6 \text{ is also } \frac{6}{10}$$

Write the correct letters to match the fractions and **decimals**.

COLUMN 1		COLUMN 2	
$\frac{34}{100}$ _D_	A) 0.60	$\frac{83}{100}$ ___	N) $\frac{61}{100}$
0.57 ___	B) $\frac{2}{10}$	$\frac{6}{10}$ ___	O) $\frac{91}{100}$
$\frac{42}{100}$ ___	C) $\frac{54}{100}$	$\frac{9}{10}$ ___	P) 0.83
$\frac{60}{100}$ ___	D) 0.34	0.91 ___	Q) 0.6
0.79 ___	E) $\frac{41}{100}$	0.64 ___	R) 0.1
0.341 ___	F) 0.98	$\frac{512}{1000}$ ___	S) $\frac{57}{100}$
0.41 ___	G) $\frac{79}{100}$	$\frac{1}{10}$ ___	T) 0.33
$\frac{27}{100}$ ___	H) 0.29	$\frac{114}{1000}$ ___	U) 0.19
$\frac{98}{100}$ ___	I) 0.42	$\frac{33}{100}$ ___	V) 0.114
$\frac{29}{100}$ ___	J) $\frac{341}{1000}$	0.57 ___	W) 0.08
0.2 ___	K) $\frac{57}{100}$	$\frac{19}{100}$ ___	X) $\frac{64}{100}$
0.7 ___	L) 0.27	$\frac{8}{100}$ ___	Y) 0.9
0.54 ___	M) $\frac{7}{10}$	0.61 ___	Z) 0.512

Challenge: Look at the prices of items in a catalog or in newspaper circular. On another sheet of paper, practice rewriting the decimal price as a fraction.

Recognizing equivalent decimals and fractions

Name:_____   Date:_____

To change a **percent** to a decimal, move the decimal point
two places to the left and drop the **percent** sign.

$$44\% = 0.44$$

Change each **percent** to a decimal.

A. 90% = _____   48% = _____   28% = _____   29% = _____   3% = _____

B. 12% = _____   64% = _____   79% = _____   24% = _____   65% = _____

C. 5% = _____   56% = _____   94% = _____   20% = _____   27% = _____

D. 17% = _____   19% = _____   82% = _____   3% = _____   72% = _____

E. 26% = _____   10% = _____   78% = _____   99% = _____   41% = _____

F. 9% = _____   4% = _____   14% = _____   36% = _____   6% = _____

Complete the table.

G.	Fractions	Decimals	Percents
H.	$\frac{1}{2}$	0.5	_____
I.	$\frac{1}{5}$	_____	20%
J.	_____	0.625	62.5%
K.	$\frac{1}{10}$	_____	_____
L.	_____	0.69	69%

Name:_____   Date:_____

Rule of Thumb: When adding or subtracting decimals, always line up the decimal points!

Add.

A.

```
     1
   0.07        01.40         2.517        01.807        51.88
   2.40        23.07        34.433        23.005        00.93
 + 13.444     + 05.19      + 12.007       00.235        05.09
 ─────────    ─────────    ──────────    + 02.069      + 00.78
  15.914
```

B.

```
                                        0.0517       0.0012       79.416
   0.008        0.017        2.450       16.0009      41.0809       0.008
  47.158        0.240        0.517        5.0018       1.7004       3.500
 + 2.009      + 23.010     + 18.560     +  7.4500    + 34.0098    + 14.980
 ─────────    ──────────   ──────────   ──────────   ──────────   ──────────
```

C.

```
   83.168       514.7890      613.004        7.009        29.0004        9.5168
 + 14.009      + 78.0045    + 528.109     + 23.870      +  7.5190     + 14.8150
 ─────────     ──────────   ──────────    ─────────     ──────────    ──────────
```

Line up the decimal points and solve.

D. 5.8001 + 41.9 = _____   0.915 + 2.0008 = _____   0.3 + .00078 = _____

E. 0.54 + 8.0040 = _____   4.5 + 12.7088 = _____

Tip:
Line up the decimal points as you rewrite the problems vertically!

Subtract.

No matter how they fall, line up the decimal points.

A.
$$51$$
  14.363   5.708   0.407
– 0.324   – 1.416   – 0.324
  14.039

B.
  32.426   12.0076   51.709
– 14.018   – 0.4581   – 23.416

C.
  51.006   0.8377   0.0138   6.527   9.00   0.96
– 4.860   – 0.0451   – 0.0060   – 5.139   – 3.36   – 0.19

D.
  8.00   7.00149   5.1870   12.0041   11.000   0.869
– 1.98   – 2.46000   – 0.4080   – 4.6980   – 3.149   – 0.476

Line up the decimal points and solve.

E. 6.03 – 0.49 = _____   23.7 – 4.092 = _____   14.907 – 0.989 = _____

F. 3.410 – 0.891 = _____   12 – 0.0189 = _____

Tip:
Line up the decimal points as you rewrite the problems vertically!

Keeping Track of **Decimal Points**:

83.4	1	There is 1 digit to the right of the **decimal point**.
x .12	+ 2	There are 2 digits to the right of the **decimal point**.
1668	3	There are 3 digits to the right of the **decimal point**.
+ 834↓		
10.008		There is a total of 3 digits to the right of the **decimal point** in the product.

Multiply.

A.
```
   14.6        18.36         7.89        91.04        0.075        0.516
 x  0.7      x    1.6      x  1.40     x  9.00      x  1.07      x 0.14
```

B.
```
  0.003        0.415         0.12        1.006         0.32       10.147
 x   .51      x    .71      x   .56     x 0.98       x 0.517      x .076
```

C.
```
  0.256      0.00124       0.4196       0.0681        0.616        1.519
 x  .145     x   .432      x  .981      x  .391      x   .51      x  .35
```

D.
```
   12.5        9.710       3.0058        15.98        1.209        1.097
 x  5.9      x    .02      x  .539      x 2.09       x 8.159      x 0.07
```

Name:_____   Date:_____

Tip:
Don't forget to add the decimal point to your answer. It belongs above the decimal point in the equation!

Divide.

A. $3\overline{)3.9}$ with work shown: quotient 1.3, -3, 9, -9 $5\overline{)5.4}$ $3\overline{)7.29}$ $5\overline{)37.5}$ $8\overline{)88.8}$ $7\overline{)6.37}$

B. $9\overline{)40.5}$ $3\overline{)2.25}$ $7\overline{)6.51}$ $2\overline{)9.22}$ $5\overline{)102.7}$ $2\overline{)4.42}$

C. $3\overline{)4.41}$ $2\overline{)9.87}$ $2\overline{)7.9}$ $3\overline{)9.6}$ $6\overline{)24.0}$ $9\overline{)80.1}$

D. $8\overline{)65.2}$ $4\overline{)25.6}$ $4\overline{)2.96}$ $8\overline{)36.2}$ $4\overline{)1.6}$ $7\overline{)8.05}$

E. $2\overline{)66.3}$ $2\overline{)9.68}$ $5\overline{)40.5}$ $8\overline{)48.2}$ $5\overline{)2.5}$ $6\overline{)7.2}$

Watch out! These problems have decimals in the divisor!

$1.6 \overline{)9.6}$

1.6 × 10 = 16.0   First, convert the divisor into a whole number
9.6 × 10 = 96.0   by multiplying the divisor and dividend by 10.

—————— decimal point

$16 \overline{)96.0}$ → 6.0
96

Next, place the decimal point in the quotient and divide as with whole numbers.

Divide.

A. $3.2 \overline{)2.24}$ $2.8 \overline{)4.48}$ $8.2 \overline{)229.6}$ $0.05 \overline{)42.5}$ $1.1 \overline{)5.5}$ $0.18 \overline{)6.3}$

B. $2.7 \overline{)22.41}$ $0.13 \overline{)0.026}$ $0.6 \overline{)806.4}$ $1.2 \overline{)0.876}$ $0.02 \overline{).158}$ $0.16 \overline{)0.624}$

C. $4.9 \overline{)2.499}$ $0.91 \overline{)6.734}$ $8.7 \overline{)53.244}$ $0.04 \overline{)0.2528}$ $0.3 \overline{)9}$ $0.8 \overline{)0.4168}$

D. $0.5 \overline{)3.125}$ $3.3 \overline{)13.86}$ $0.7 \overline{)5.32}$ $0.3 \overline{)0.192}$ $0.005 \overline{)6.3}$ $6.3 \overline{)9.765}$

Name:_____   Date:_____

Review: Adding & Subtracting Decimals

Add or subtract.

A.
$$\begin{array}{r} 6.234 \\ + 5.292 \\ \hline \end{array}$$
$$\begin{array}{r} 25.159 \\ + 67.987 \\ \hline \end{array}$$
$$\begin{array}{r} 0.25 \\ + 45.96 \\ \hline \end{array}$$
$$\begin{array}{r} 0.98 \\ + 1.57 \\ \hline \end{array}$$
$$\begin{array}{r} 5.50 \\ + 6.74 \\ \hline \end{array}$$

B.
$$\begin{array}{r} 12.589 \\ - 7.621 \\ \hline \end{array}$$
$$\begin{array}{r} 74.25 \\ - 49.02 \\ \hline \end{array}$$
$$\begin{array}{r} 6.555 \\ - 5.666 \\ \hline \end{array}$$
$$\begin{array}{r} 0.549 \\ - 0.026 \\ \hline \end{array}$$
$$\begin{array}{r} 12.00 \\ - 7.25 \\ \hline \end{array}$$

C.
$$\begin{array}{r} 1.230 \\ 5.970 \\ + 0.046 \\ \hline \end{array}$$
$$\begin{array}{r} 16.579 \\ 0.049 \\ + 22.147 \\ \hline \end{array}$$
$$\begin{array}{r} 52.052 \\ 25.255 \\ + 0.052 \\ \hline \end{array}$$
$$\begin{array}{r} 13.630 \\ 8.241 \\ + 12.033 \\ \hline \end{array}$$
$$\begin{array}{r} 18.230 \\ 4.756 \\ + 11.020 \\ \hline \end{array}$$

D.
$$\begin{array}{r} 65.98 \\ - 59.74 \\ \hline \end{array}$$
$$\begin{array}{r} 102.02 \\ - 32.01 \\ \hline \end{array}$$
$$\begin{array}{r} 75.369 \\ - 25.090 \\ \hline \end{array}$$
$$\begin{array}{r} 15.246 \\ - 9.459 \\ \hline \end{array}$$
$$\begin{array}{r} 245.300 \\ - 14.253 \\ \hline \end{array}$$

E. $15.023 + 0.698 =$ $0.589 + 0.987 =$ $0.123 + 12.344 =$

F. $15.239 - 7.245 =$ $56.999 - 5.789 =$ $0.985 - 0.561 =$

Name:_____   Date:_____

Review: Multiplying & Dividing Decimals

Solve each equation below.

A.	4.35 x 0.26	7.563 x 1.360	6.92 x .06	2.549 x 1.050	0.236 x 0.540
B.	13.045 x 2.135	14.98 x 1.95	22.593 x .044	45.23 x 2.361	55.25 x 4.12
C.	8⟌0.032	2⟌9.204	3⟌7.89	4⟌6.044	5⟌0.565
D.	.04⟌24.24	0.6⟌36.066	1.2⟌2.46	.15⟌30.30	2.6⟌52.078

STOP! TAKE A BREAK! You did a great job! Place your Book Mark here & RELAX!

Name:_____   Date:_____

U.S. Customary Measurements of Length

12 inches (in.) = 1 foot (ft.)

3 feet = 1 yard (yd.)

5,280 feet = 1 mile (mi.)

1,760 yards = 1 mile

Convert each measurement.

A. 60 in. = _____ ft.   3 yd. = _____ in.   4 mi. = _____ in.   39 ft. = _____ in.

B. $4\frac{1}{2}$ mi. = _____ ft. $7\frac{5}{6}$ ft. = _____ in.   9 mi. = _____ yd.   13 yd. = _____ in.

C. 31 mi. = _____ yd.   1,272 in. = _____ ft.   1,512 in. = _____ yd.   1,628 ft. = _____ in.

Solve, then convert each answer to the simplest expression of length.

D.   10 ft.   7 ft. 8 in.   3 yd. 5 ft.   9 mi. 870 ft.
   +   3 ft. 11 in.   + 8 ft. 4 in.   + 7 yd. 8 ft.   + 11 mi. 4,000 ft.

Tip:
Think of each equation like a decimal. Example: 4 yd. 6ft. = 4.6

E.   4 yd. 2 ft.   36 ft. 9 in.   14 yd. 4 ft.   18 mi. 178 ft.   19 yd. 3 in.
   – 2 yd. 1 ft.   – 18 ft. 6 in.   – 9 yd. 3 ft.   – 1 mi. 62 ft.   – 12 yd. 10 in.

Solve. Circle your answers.

1. Mrs. Gibson's class measured the heights of its three tallest students. Emily is five-feet four-inches tall, Blaine is five-feet tall, and William is four-feet 11 inches tall. What is the combined height of these three students?

2. There are two mountains in the town of Okeene. One is three-miles 2,480-feet high, and the other is one-mile 5,170-feet high. What is the difference in the heights?

Understanding measurements of length

45

Name:_____ Date:_____

Write the unit of measurement that makes the most sense.

U.S. Customary Measurements of Liquid	U.S. Customary Measurements of Weight
1 pint (pt.) = 2 cups (c.) 1 quart (qt.) = 2 pints 1 gallon (gal.) = 4 quarts	16 ounces (oz.) = 1 pound (lb.) 2,000 pounds = 1 ton (T.)

Write the correct unit of measure.

1. a small juice box weighs 1 _____   a mouse weighs 5 _____

2. a basketball weighs 7 _____   a bicycle weighs 28 _____

3. a truck weighs 2 _____   a container of yogurt holds 1 _____

4. a horse trailer weighs 1 _____   a canoe weighs 90 _____

5. a bag of potatoes weighs 5 _____   an apple weighs 5 _____

6. a set of pens weighs 4 _____   a swimming pool holds 1,200 _____

7. a compact disc weighs 4 _____   a flashlight weighs 2 _____

8. a washing machine holds 15 _____   clothes in the washing machine weigh 20 _____

Convert each measurement.

A. 6 qt. = _____ c.   9 pt. = _____ c.   3 gal. = _____ c.   14 qt. = _____ c.

B. 16 gal. = _____ pt.   23 qt. = _____ pt.   50 gal. = _____ c.   36 qt. = _____ pt.

C. 96 oz. = _____ lb.   132 lb. = _____ oz.   18 lb. = _____ oz.   3 T. = _____ lb.

D. 1.8 T. = _____ oz.   48 oz. = _____ lb.   1 T 16 lb. = _____ oz.   4,000 lb. = _____ T.

E. 34 gal. = _____ pt.   4,000 gal. = _____ qt.   346 lb. = _____ oz.   561 qt. = _____ pt.

Understanding measurements of liquid and weight

Name:_____ Date:_____

Metric Units for Measuring Weight	**Metric Units for Measuring Liquids**
1000 milligrams (mg) = 1 gram (g) 1000 grams (g) = 1 kilograms (kg) 1000 kilograms (kg) = 1 metric ton (T)	1000 milliliters (mL) = 1 Liter (L)

Metric Units for Linear Measures

10 millimeters (mm) = 1 centimeter (cm)
100 centimeters (cm) = 1 meter (m)
1000 meters (m) = 1 kilometer (km)

Challenge: Measure an object in inches and in centimeters. How do they compare? Can you use inches and centimeters at the same time?

Write the unit of measurement that makes the most sense.

1. The width of your fingernail is 1 _____.   A dime is about 1 _____ thick.

2. The diameter of a CD or DVD is 12 _____.   A bottle of soda holds 2 _____.

3. A nickel weighs 5 _____.

4. The length of an Olympic-size swimming pool is _____.

Convert each measurement.

A. 9 cm = _____ mm   2 L = _____ mL   7000 g = _____ kg

B. 3 km = _____ m   4000 mg = _____ g   5000 mL = _____ L

C. 7 g = _____ mg   2000 m = _____ km   6000 m = _____ km

D. 4 L = _____ mL   80 mm = _____ cm   1 m = _____ mm

E. 8000 g = _____ kg   400 cm = _____ m   8 kg = _____ g

F. 4 g = _____ mg   5000 kg = _____ T   3 m = _____ cm

G. 8 L = _____ mL   4 km = _____ cm   2 T = _____ kg

Name:_____ Date:_____

Write the correct letter to match the geometric term to its definition.

1. Quadrilateral _____   A) part of a line between two end points, an exact location

2. Parallelogram _____   B) a polygon with four sides

3. Point _____   C) a polygon with eight sides

4. Right angle _____   D) a ten-sided polygon

5. Acute angle _____   E) a never-ending path in the opposite direction with no endpoints

6. Obtuse angle _____   F) a quadrilateral whose opposite sides are parallel and congruent

7. Line _____   G) a 90° angle

8. Decagon _____   H) an angle more than 90°

9. Congruent _____   I) an angle less than 90°

10. Octagon _____   J) having the same size and shape

11. Pentagon _____   K) a polygon with five sides and angles

12. Heptagon _____   L) lines and/or line segments that are exactly the same distance apart

13. Nonagon _____   M) a polygon with six sides and angles

14. Dodecagon _____   N) two lines that intersect to form four right angles

15. Hexagon _____   O) a polygon with twelve sides and angles

16. Rotation _____   P) a polygon with nine sides and angles

17. Translation _____   Q) sliding a figure in any direction

18. Reflection _____   R) turning a figure around a point

19. Parallel _____   S) a polygon with seven sides and angles

20. Perpendicular _____   T) when a figure is flipped over a line

Understanding geometric terms

angle ABC or <ABC

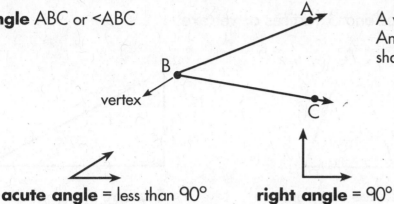

A vertex is an endpoint shared by two rays. An **angle** is made up of two rays that share a common endpoint.

 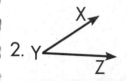 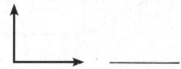 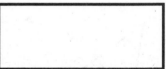

acute angle = less than 90°   **right angle** = 90°   **obtuse angle** = more than 90°

Name each **angle**. Then, circle the letter that stands for its **vertex**.

1. 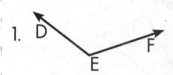 ☐

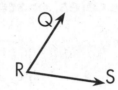 ☐

2.  ☐

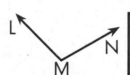 ☐

Write **acute**, **obtuse**, or **right** to identify each **angle**.

3. 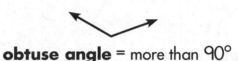 _____    _____    _____

4. 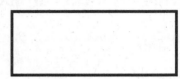 _____   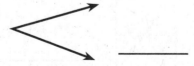 _____    _____

5. 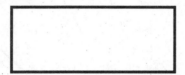 _____   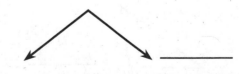 _____   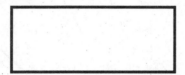 _____

Complete each sentence.

6. An angle measuring less than 90° is called _____.

7. An angle measuring more than 90° is called _____.

8. An angle measuring exactly 90° is called _____.

A **triangle** is a polygon with 3 sides and 3 vertices or vertexes.

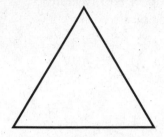  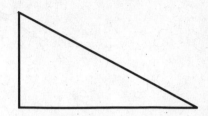

Equilateral triangles have 3 sides of equal length.

Isosceles triangles have 2 sides of equal length.

Scalene triangles have no sides of equal length.

Write **equilateral**, **isosceles**, or **scalene** to identify each **triangle**.

1. 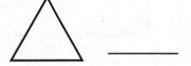 _____   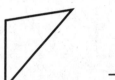 _____   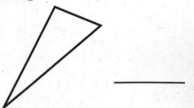 _____

2. 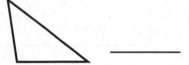 _____   _____   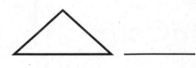 _____

3.  _____   _____   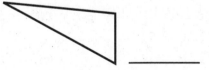 _____

4. 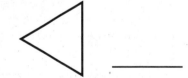 _____    _____   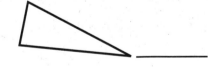 _____

5. 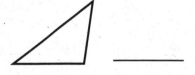 _____   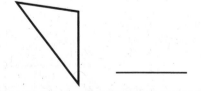 _____   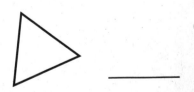 _____

Complete each sentence.

6. A triangle with no sides of equal length is called _____.

7. A triangle with two sides of equal length is called _____.

8. A triangle with three sides of equal length is called _____.

Name:_____ Date:_____

Review: Measurement

Match each object to its correct measurement.

1. eyedropper   liter   bowl of soup   quart

2. carton of milk   gram   punch bowl   gallon

3. paper clip   milliliter   bucket of paint   pint

Ready to measure!

Circle the correct answer.

4. How many inches is 6 feet 9 inches?

   a) 86   b) 81   c) 89   d) 90

5. How many feet are there in one yard?

   a) 3   b) 30   c) 100   d) 10

6. When you are converting larger units to smaller units, you:

   a) divide   b) multiply   c) add   d) subtract

7. When you are converting smaller units to larger units, you:

   a) divide   b) multiply   c) add   d) subtract

Challenge: Make a list of all the units of the Metric System and the units of the U.S. Customary System. Write the conversion of 1 metric unit to the equivalent customary units.

---

8. Draw the following.

a line that is 5 centimeters long	a square measuring $1\frac{1}{2}$ inch on all sides
a line that is $3\frac{1}{4}$ inches long	

Name:_____   Date:_____

Review: Geometry

Use the picture to answer the following questions.

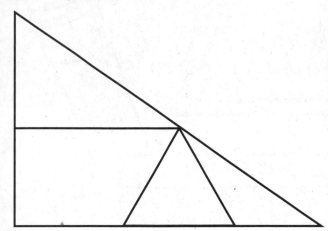

1. How many right angles are there?

   _____

2. How many obtuse angles are there?

   _____

3. How many acute angles are there?

   _____

4. How many equilateral triangles are there?

   _____

5. How many isosceles triangles are there?

   _____

6. How many scalene triangles are there?

   _____

Name each polygon.

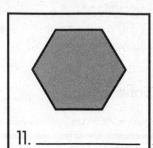

7. _____

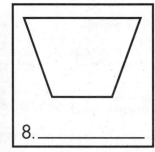

8. _____

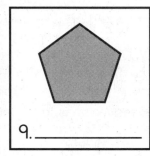

9. _____

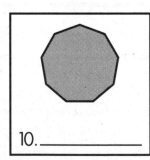

10. _____

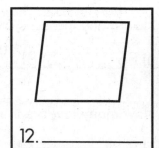

11. _____

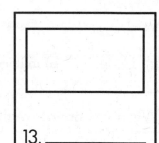

12. _____

13. _____

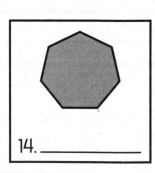

14. _____

STOP! TAKE A BREAK! You did a great job! Place your Book Mark here & RELAX!

Name:_____ Date:_____

Test Scores
100 87 70 95 88 90 60 100

Mean: 86
Median: 89
Mode: 100

Mean is another word for average.
Median is the middle number in a group of numbers in order.
Test scores: 60 70 87 88 **89** 90 95 100 100
Mode is the number that appears the most often.

Find the **mean**, **median**, and **mode** for each.

Basketball Points
6 22 12 36 19

Golf Scores
93 70 90 90 68 75

1. **Mean:** _____

   Median: _____

   Mode: _____

2. **Mean:** _____

   Median: _____

   Mode: _____

	Data	mean	median	mode
A.	10, 17, 10, 14, 19			
B.	18, 19, 64, 19, 32, 60, 61			
C.	11, 38, 13, 38, 40			
D.	12, 15, 11, 15, 13, 10, 15			
E.	87, 81, 95, 79, 83, 79			
F.	96, 62, 97, 100, 96, 87, 85			

Tip:
The first two letters in **mode**
are **mo** = **m**ost **o**ften. Also, **median**
means middle – the median of
a highway separates traffic in
the middle.

Name:_____ Date:_____/_____

Answer each question using a number and a fraction. Circle your answers.

What's the Probability?

1. Maggie has a bag of marbles with eight purple marbles, five orange marbles, four blue, and seven green. How many marbles does Maggie have in all?

   $(8 + 5 + 4 + 7) = $ (24).

   What are Maggie's chances of picking a blue marble?
   Her chances of picking a blue marble are 4 in 24 or $\frac{4}{24}$.

2. Jesse is trying to draw a queen from a deck of 52 playing cards. If he already drew one card with no luck, what is the **probability** of him drawing a queen now?

   What is the **probability** of drawing a queen on the third try if a queen hasn't been drawn yet?

3. If there are nine boys and 13 girls in the gym class and a student closes his eyes to pick a person for his team, is he more likely to pick a boy or a girl?

   What are the chances of picking a boy?

   What are the chances of picking a girl?

4. Penny's large pack of gum contains five strawberry-flavored pieces, three lime-flavored pieces, and eight lemon-flavored pieces. If Penny pulls out a piece without looking, what flavor is she most likely to get?

   What are the **probabilities** of each flavor being chosen?

5. A bag of colorful shelled candy contains eight orange, four green, seven yellow, three blue, six red, and seven brown pieces.
   What is the **probability** of drawing a green or yellow piece of candy?

   What is the **probability** of drawing an orange or blue piece?

   Which color candy is likely to be drawn?

6. A dart board has 14 spaces that show even numbers between 3 and 31 and ten spaces that show odd numbers from 3 to 21. What is the **probability** of a dart landing on a space with a prime number?

   What is the **probability** of a dart landing on a space with a composite number?

A **power** is the product of multiplying a number by itself. It is represented as a **base number** and an **exponent**.
The **base number** indicates what number is being multiplied, and the **exponent** indicates how many times the base number is to be multiplied.

$$10^5 = 10 \times 10 \times 10 \times 10 \times 10 = 100,000$$

base number ←———┘   └——→ factors   ———→ exponent

Write the factors, then find the value.

A. $5^2 =$ $7^3 =$ $9^3 =$ $3^4 =$ $2^3 =$
   $5 \times 5 = 25$

B. $10^6 =$ $10^4 =$ $5^4 =$ $6^6 =$ $3^5 =$

Write the value.

C. $7^2 = 49$ $9^5 =$ $4^4 =$ $2^5 =$ $1^9 =$

D. $8^1 =$ $3^2 =$ $2^7 =$ $3^4 =$ $8^2 =$

Write the value using **exponents**.

E. $5 \times 5 \times 5 \times 5 \times 5 =$ $10 \times 10 \times 10 \times 10 =$ $6 \times 6 \times 6 \times 6 =$ $2 \times 2 =$

F. $4 \times 4 \times 4 \times 4 =$ $7 \times 7 \times 7 =$ $2 \times 2 \times 2 \times 2 \times 2 =$ $3 \times 3 \times 3 =$

G. $10 \times 10 \times 10 =$ $5 \times 5 =$ $8 \times 8 \times 8 =$ $10 \times 10 =$

Fill in the missing numbers.

	Product	Number to Given Power	Standard Notation
H.	$8 \times 8 \times 8$	8^3	512
I.	5×5		
J.		12^3	
K.	$2 \times 2 \times 2 \times 2 \times 2$		

The **square** of a number is the number times itself.

$$5^2 = 5 \times 5 = 25$$

The **cube** of a number is the number multiplied twice by itself.

$$5^3 = 5 \times 5 \times 5 = 125$$

Write the **square** or **cube** of each number.

A. $4^2 =$ ___4 x 4 = 16___ $9^2 =$ _____ $3^3 =$ _____

B. $6^3 =$ _____ $7^2 =$ _____ $15^3 =$ _____

C. $10^3 =$ _____ $5^3 =$ _____ $14^2 =$ _____

D. $20^2 =$ _____ $24^3 =$ _____ $19^3 =$ _____

E. $8^3 =$ _____ $13^2 =$ _____ $48^2 =$ _____

F. $17^2 =$ _____ $25^3 =$ _____ $37^2 =$ _____

Write the **square** root.

G. 36 = _6^2_ 64 = ____ 81 = ____ 25 = ____ 324 = ____ 529 = ____

H. 100 = ____ 49 = ____ 4 = ____ 16 = ____ 121 = ____ 1,600 = ____

I. 400 = ____ 225 = ____ 625 = ____ 144 = ____ 900 = ____ 2,500 = ____

Write the **cube** root.

J. 125 = _5^3_ 1,000 = ____ 64 = ____ 27 = ____ 8 = ____ 216 = ____

K. 512 = ____ 1,728 = ____ 2,744 = ____ 343 = ____ 8,000 = ____ 6,859 = ____

Name:_____ Date:_____

Let's change the fraction $\frac{5}{8}$ to a **percent**.

1st: Change the fraction to a decimal.

Divide the numerator by the denominator.
Add 0's to keep from having a remainder.

$$\begin{array}{r} 0.625 \\ 8\overline{)5.000} \\ -48 \\ \hline 20 \\ -16 \\ \hline 40 \\ -40 \\ \hline 0 \end{array}$$

A percent means per hundred. So... 25% means 25 of 100.

2nd: Move the decimal point two places to the right and add the **percent** sign.

.62,5%

Change each fraction to a **percent**. Don't forget the **percent** sign.

A. $\frac{80}{100}$ = _____ $\frac{3}{4}$ = _____ $\frac{3}{8}$ = _____ $\frac{9}{10}$ = _____ $\frac{3}{19}$ = _____

B. $\frac{22}{100}$ = _____ $\frac{4}{5}$ = _____ $\frac{9}{20}$ = _____ $\frac{4}{25}$ = _____ $\frac{9}{100}$ = _____

C. $\frac{3}{5}$ = _____ $\frac{6}{25}$ = _____ $\frac{7}{15}$ = _____ $\frac{16}{25}$ = _____ $\frac{7}{8}$ = _____

D. $\frac{5}{9}$ = _____ $\frac{4}{50}$ = _____ $\frac{8}{15}$ = _____ $\frac{3}{10}$ = _____ $\frac{2}{5}$ = _____

E. $\frac{8}{25}$ = _____ $\frac{11}{50}$ = _____ $\frac{11}{12}$ = _____ $\frac{9}{25}$ = _____ $\frac{1}{5}$ = _____

Challenge: See how many things you can list that can be shown in **percents**. For example, test scores can be shown in **percents**.

Name:_____   Date:_____

Reasonableness is working a problem to find the answer that makes the most sense.

Write the ages.

1. I am five years younger than Patty, who will be 46 in seven years.

   My age: _____   Patty's age: _____

2. Kim is 52 years younger than her grandpa, who will be 98 in 14 years.

   Kim's age: _____   Grandpa's age: _____

3. Syd is seven years older than Kathy, who will be 19 in eight years.

   Syd's age: _____   Kathy's age: _____

4. Dale is 19 years younger than Ann, who will be 46 in 23 years.

   Dale's age: _____   Ann's age: _____

The pie chart shows the way Lucy spends her monthly income of $300. Use the chart to answer the questions.

5. What is a reasonable estimate of the amount of money Lucy spends on groceries? _____

6. What is a reasonable estimate of the amount of money Lucy spends on gas? _____

7. About how much does she spend on entertainment each month? _____

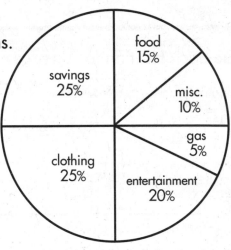

savings 25%   food 15%   misc. 10%   gas 5%   entertainment 20%   clothing 25%

The chart below shows the percentages of the fifth and sixth grade students who named their favorite flavor of ice cream.

Ice Cream Flavor	%
Chocolate	30%
Chocolate Chip	38%
Vanilla	2%
Strawberry	9%
Cookies-and-Cream	11%
Butter Pecan	10%

8. If there are 370 students in fifth and sixth grade, what is the reasonable number of students who like chocolate chip?

9. What is the reasonable number of students who like strawberry or cookies-and-cream?

10. Choose three flavors which make up exactly half of the total percentage.

11. What is a reasonable ratio of students who chose chocolate to butter pecan?

Name:_____   Date:_____

Review: Mixed Facts

1. Write the **square** of each number.

9^2 32^2 20^2 65^2 14^2

____   ____   ____   ____   ____

2. Find the **mean** of these numbers:

94, 96, 98, 76, 84, 86, 82, 88

a) 83   b) 88   c). 92   d) 90

3. Joey has a bag containing 15 blue marbles, 19 red marbles, and 8 yellow marbles. If Joey pulls one marble out of the bag without looking, what is the **probability** that he will get a yellow marble on the first try?

What is the **probability** that he will pull out a yellow marble on the second try (with one marble already removed)?

4. Find the **mode** of these numbers:

17, 14, 22, 17, 36, 14, 23, 17, 33, 11

5. Shade 25% of this rectangle.

6. Change each **fraction** to **percents**.

$\dfrac{7}{20}$ = _____

$\dfrac{4}{5}$ = _____

$\dfrac{7}{8}$ = _____

7. Write the **square root**.

144 = ____   25 = ____   121 = ____

625 = ____   1600 = ____   529 = ____

8. Which factors represent $3^3 \times 2^3 \times 5$?

a) 6 x 9 x 5

b) 3 x 2 x 2 x 2 x 5

c) 3 x 3 x 3 x 2 x 2 x 2 x 5

d) 6 x 5

9. Kenny and Joe caught a total of 18 fish. Kenny caught six more fish than Joe. How many fish did each of them catch?

10. The **mean** of a group of numbers is also known as the _____ of a group of numbers.

Name:_____ Date:_____

Review: Mixed Facts

---

1. Match the percent to the fraction.

$\dfrac{3}{4}$ 0.8

$\dfrac{1}{5}$ 0.75

$\dfrac{9}{100}$ 0.09

$\dfrac{3}{10}$ 0.2

$\dfrac{4}{5}$ 0.3

6. Write the value of each number.

$10^3 =$ $3^3 =$ $8^4 =$

$10^2 =$ $2^5 =$ $9^4 =$

$10^5 =$ $6^3 =$ $7^3 =$

2. Abby has 5 pairs of socks all mixed up in her drawer. Each pair is a different color: red, pink, yellow, purple, and orange. What is the **probability** that she will pick out one pink sock on her first try? What about her second try?

7. What percent of this shape is shaded?

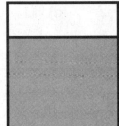

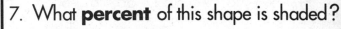

3. Find the **mode** in this group of numbers:

55, 89, 74, 56, 89, 74, 12, 54, 74, 63, 63

8. Write the **square root** of the following numbers.

225 = _____   144 = _____   289 = _____

4. Dan is 14 years younger than Bob, who will be 43 in 17 years. What are their ages now?

Dan's age _____   Bob's age _____

9. Write the **cube root** of the following numbers.

64 = _____   216 = _____   1000 = _____

5. Find the **median** of these numbers:

24, 56, 87, 12, 64, 45, 82, 34, 19

10. Find the **mean** of these numbers:

10, 20, 30, 40, 50, 60, 70, 80, 90

STOP! TAKE A BREAK! You did a great job!
Place your Book Mark here & RELAX!

Answer Key

Please take time to review the work your child or student has completed. Remember to praise both success and effort. If your child makes a mistake, let him or her know that mistakes are a part of learning. Explain why the incorrect response was not the best choice. Then, encourage your child to think it through and select a better choice.

page 3

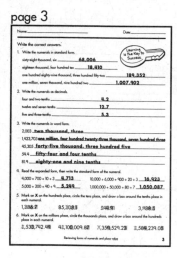

page 4

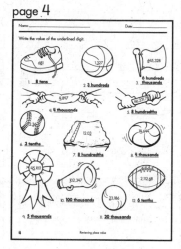

page 5

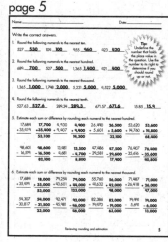

page 6

page 7

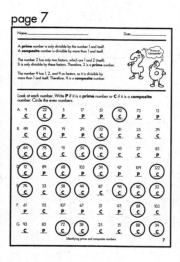

page 8

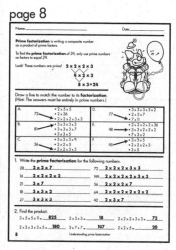

page 9

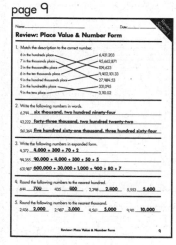

page 10

page 11

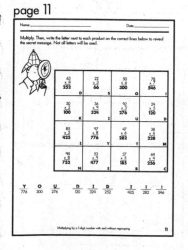

page 12

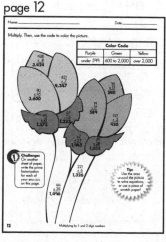

page 13

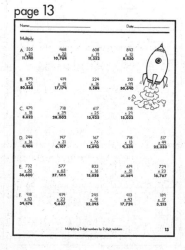

page 14

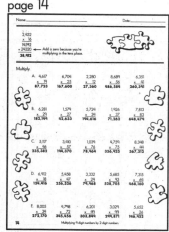

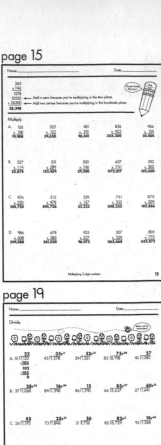

page 15

Multiply.

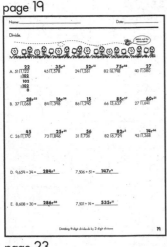

page 16

Divide. Then, draw a line to the matching quotients.

page 17

Divide.

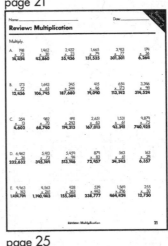

page 18

Divide. Then, use the code to solve the riddle.

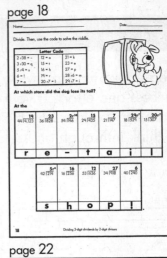

At which store did the dog lose its tail?

At the

r e - t a i l

s h o p !

page 19

Divide.

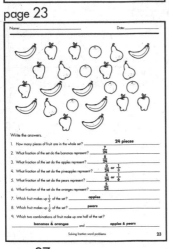

page 20

Read each problem. Then, divide or multiply to solve it.

1. Johnny needs to buy chicken for a Mexican fiesta. He can buy seven packages of chicken for $26.25. How much does each package of chicken cost?

$3.75

2. Katie needs two cucumbers for a salad. She bought two cucumbers for $2.55. What is the cost per cucumber?

$0.51

3. A grocery store clerk stocked cereal boxes in rows of 40 across on a shelf. He made six rows of boxes. How many boxes of cereal were stacked in all?

240 boxes

4. Mrs. Smith buys three cases of juice boxes for her fifth grade class. Each case costs $2.50 and contains 12 juice boxes. How much does Mrs. Smith pay for all the juice?

$7.50

5. Julie and her friends go to the store. Julie has $40.00 that she wants to share equally with her seven friends. How much money does each girl get?

$5.00

6. Abbey and her friends decide to buy five bags of candy. There were 45 pieces of candy in each bag. What is the total number of pieces that Abbey and her friends shared?

225 pieces of candy

page 21

Multiply.

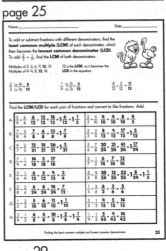

page 22

Multiply.

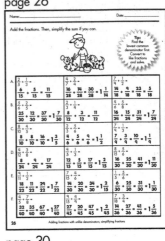

page 23

Write the answers.

1. How many pieces of fruit are in the whole set? **24 pieces**
2. What fraction of the set do the bananas represent?
3. What fraction of the set do the apples represent?
4. What fraction of the set do the pineapples represent?
5. What fraction of the set do the oranges represent?
6. What fraction of the set do the oranges represent?
7. Which fruit makes up ⅓ of the set? **apples**
8. Which fruit makes up ¼ of the set? **pears**
9. Which two combinations of fruit make up one half of the set? **bananas & oranges** **apples & pears**

page 24

Find the sum or difference in its simplest form.

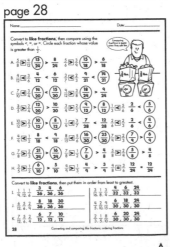

Solve the problems.

1. Carla walked ⅓ of a mile on Monday, ⅔ mile on Tuesday, and ⅔ of a mile on Wednesday. How far did Carla walk in all? **2 ⅓ miles**

2. Joey swam the butterfly stroke for ⅞ of a mile and freestyle for ⅝ of a mile. How far did Joey swim in all? **1 ½ miles**

3. On Tuesday, Olivia and her friend pedaled 2 ¾ of a mile. Wednesday, they increased their mileage by 2 ¼ of a mile. How far did they pedal over both days? **7 yards**

4. This winter Jenny bought fabric for two dresses. One dress required 3 ¾ yards of fabric and the other called for 5 ½ yards. How much fabric did Jenny buy in all? **8 ¾ yards**

page 25

To add or subtract fractions with different denominators, find the **least common multiple (LCM)** of each denominator, which then becomes the **lowest common denominator (LCD)**.

Find the LCM/LCD for each pair of fractions and convert to like fractions. Add.

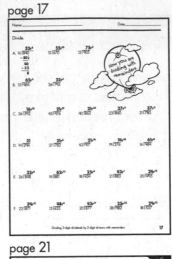

page 26

Add the fractions. Then, simplify the sum if you can.

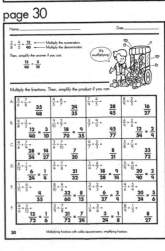

page 27

Add and subtract the fractions. Then, simplify the answer if you can.

page 28

Convert to **like fractions**, then compare using the symbols <, >, or =. Circle each fraction whose value is greater than ½.

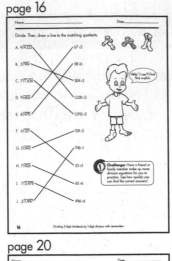

Convert to **like fractions**, then put them in order from least to greatest.

page 29

To add mixed numerals, find the lowest common denominator. Then, add the whole number and the numerators.

To subtract mixed numerals, find the lowest common denominator, too. Sometimes, you will need to regroup.

Solve the problems.

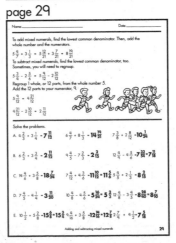

page 30

Multiply the fractions. Then, simplify the product if you can.

Answers

page 47
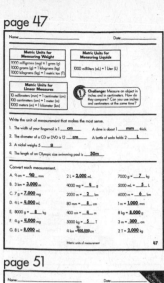

Metric Units for Measuring Weight
1000 milligrams (mg) = 1 gram (g)
1000 grams (g) = 1 kilogram (kg)
1000 kilograms (kg) = 1 metric ton (t)

Metric Units for Measuring Liquids
1000 milliliters (mL) = 1 Liter (L)

Metric Units for Linear Measures
10 millimeters (mm) = 1 centimeter (cm)
100 centimeters (cm) = 1 meter (m)
1000 meters (m) = 1 kilometer (km)

Write the unit of measurement that makes the most sense.
1. The width of your fingernail is 1 __cm__.
2. The diameter of a CD or DVD is 12 __cm__.
3. A nickel weighs 5 __g__.
4. The length of an Olympic size swimming pool is __50m__.

Convert each measurement.
A. 9 cm = __90__ mm   2 L = __2,000__ mL   7000 g = __7__ kg
B. 3 km = __3,000__ m   4000 mg = __4__ g   5000 mL = __5__ L
C. 7 g = __7,000__ mg   2000 m = __2__ km   6000 m = __6__ km
D. 4 L = __4,000__ mL   80 mm = __8__ cm   1 m = __1,000__ mm
E. 8000 g = __8__ kg   400 cm = __4__ m   8 kg = __8,000__ g
F. 4 g = __4,000__ mg   5000 kg = __5__ t   3 m = __300__ cm
G. 8 L = __8,000__ mL   4 km = __400,000__ cm   2 T = __2,000__ kg

page 48

Write the correct letter to match the geometric term to its definition.
1. Quadrilateral __B__
2. Parallelogram __F__
3. Point __A__
4. Right angle __G__
5. Acute angle __I__
6. Obtuse angle __H__
7. Line __E__
8. Decagon __D__
9. Congruent __J__
10. Octagon __O__
11. Pentagon __K__
12. Heptagon __S__
13. Nonagon __P__
14. Dodecagon __Q__
15. Hexagon __M__
16. Rotation __R__
17. Translation __L__
18. Reflection __T__
19. Parallel __C__
20. Perpendicular __N__

page 49
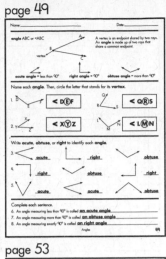

angle ABC or ∠ABC

acute angle – less than 90°   right angle = 90°   obtuse angle – more than 90°

Name each angle. Then, circle the letter that stands for its vertex.

Write acute, obtuse, or right to identify each angle.

Complete each sentence.
6. An angle measuring less than 90° is called __an acute angle__.
7. An angle measuring more than 90° is called __an obtuse angle__.
8. An angle measuring exactly 90° is called __a right angle__.

page 50
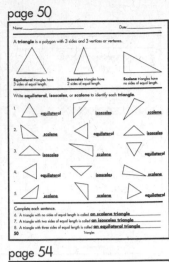

A **triangle** is a polygon with 3 sides and 3 vertices or vertexes.

Equilateral triangles have 3 sides of equal length.
Isosceles triangles have 2 sides of equal length.
Scalene triangles have no sides of equal length.

Write equilateral, isosceles, or scalene to identify each triangle.

Complete each sentence.
6. A triangle with no sides of equal length is called __an scalene triangle__.
7. A triangle with two sides of equal length is called __an isosceles triangle__.
8. A triangle with three sides of equal length is called __an equilateral triangle__.

page 51
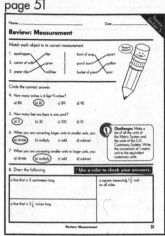

Review: Measurement

Match each object to its correct measurement.
1. eyedropper
2. carton of milk
3. paper clip
bowl of soup – quart
punch bowl – gallon
bucket of paint

Circle the correct answer.
4. How many inches is 6 feet 9 inches?
5. How many feet are there in one yard? 3
6. When you are converting larger units to smaller units, you — divide
7. When you are converting smaller units to larger units, you — multiply
8. Draw the following.

page 52
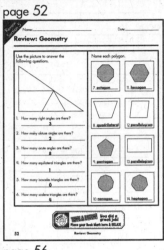

Review: Geometry

Use the picture to answer the following questions.
Name each polygon.
7. octagon
8. quadrilateral
9. pentagon
10. nonagon
11. hexagon
12. parallelogram
13. parallelogram
14. heptagon

1. How many right angles are there?
2. How many obtuse angles are there?
3. How many acute angles are there?
4. How many equilateral triangles are there?
5. How many isosceles triangles are there?
6. How many scalene triangles are there?

page 53

Test Scores	Mean: 86
100 87 70 95 88 90 60 100	Median: 89 Mode: 100

Mean is another word for average.
Median is the middle number in a group of numbers in order.
Mode is the number that appears the most often.

Data	mean	median	mode
A. 10, 17, 10, 19, 19	14	14	10
B. 18, 74, 64, 19, 32, 60, 61	39	32	19
C. 11, 38, 13, 38, 40	28	38	38
D. 12, 15, 11, 15, 13, 10, 15	13	13	15
E. 87, 81, 95, 79, 83, 79	84	82	79
F. 96, 62, 97, 100, 96, 87, 85	89	96	96

page 54

Answer each question using a number and a fraction. Circle your answers.

What's the Probability?

page 55
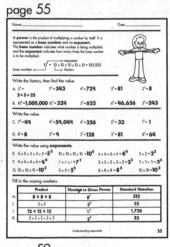

A **power** is the product of multiplying a number by itself.

Write the factors, then find the value.

Fill in the missing numbers.

	Product	Number to Given Power	Standard Notation
H.	8 × 8 × 8	8³	512
I.	5 × 5	5²	25
J.	12 × 12 × 12	12³	1,728
K.	2 × 2 × 2 × 2 × 2		32

page 56
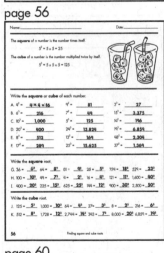

The **square** of a number is the number times itself.

The **cube** of a number is the number multiplied twice by itself.

Write the square or cube of each number.

Write the square root.

Write the cube root.

page 57
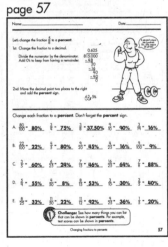

Let's change the fraction to a percent.

Change each fraction to a **percent**. Don't forget the **percent** sign.

page 58

Reasonableness is working on a problem to find the answer that makes the most sense.

Write the ages.
1. I am five years younger than Patty, who will be 46 in seven years.
2. Kim is 52 years younger than her grandpa, who will be 48 in 14 years.

The pie chart shows the way Lucy spends her monthly income of $300.

page 59

Review: Mixed Facts

1. Write the **square** of each number.
2. Find the **mean** of these numbers.
6. Change each **fraction** to percents.
7. Write the square root.

page 60
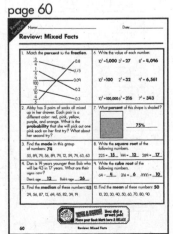

Review: Mixed Facts

1. Match the **percent** to the **fraction**.

64   Answers

page 31

page 32

page 33

Review: Fractions

page 34

Review: Fractions

page 35

page 36

page 37

page 38

page 39

page 40

page 41

page 42

page 43

Review: Adding & Subtracting Decimals

page 44

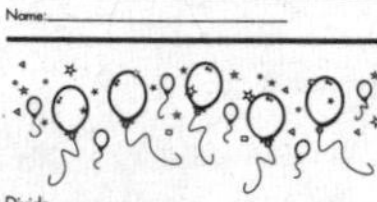

Review: Multiplying & Dividing Decimals

page 45

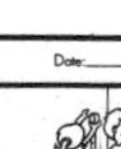

U.S. Customary Measurements of Length

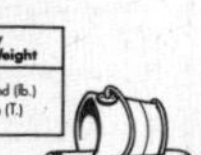

page 46